Contents

Some words are shown in bold, **like this**. You can find out what they mean by looking in the glossary.

Smoking today

Sixty years ago, lots of people smoked tobacco. More than half the men in the United Kingdom smoked, and many women did, too. Since then we have learned how dangerous smoking is. Now far fewer people smoke.

◄ Smoking was very popular in the 1950s.

Tough Topics

Tobacco

Ana Deboo

www.raintreepublishers.co.uk
Visit our website to find out
more information about
Raintree books.

To order:
☎ Phone 0845 6044371
🖶 Fax +44 (0) 1865 312263
🖳 Email myorders@raintreepublishers.co.uk

Customers from outside the UK please telephone +44 1865 312262

Raintree is an imprint of Capstone Global Library Limited,
a company incorporated in England and Wales having its
registered office at 7 Pilgrim Street, London, EC4V 6LB –
Registered company number: 6695582

Text © Capstone Global Library Limited 2007
First published in paperback in 2008

Editorial: Charlotte Guillain
Design: Richard Parker and Q2A Solutions
Picture Research: Erica Martin and Ginny Stroud-Lewis
Production: Duncan Gilbert

Originated by Chroma Graphics (Overseas) Pte. Ltd
Printed and bound in China by South China Printing Co.Ltd

ISBN 978 0 431 90775 8 (hardback)
11 10 09 08 07
10 9 8 7 6 5 4 3 2 1

ISBN 978 0 431 90780 2 (paperback)
11
10 9 8 7 6 5 4 3 2

British Library Cataloguing in Publication Data
Deboo, Ana
Tobacco. - (Tough topics)
1. Tobacco use - Juvenile literature 2. Tobacco use -
Health aspects - Juvenile literature
I. Title
362.2'9

A full catalogue record for this book is available from the
British Library.

Acknowledgements
The author and publisher are grateful to the following for
permission to reproduce copyright material: Alamy Images
pp. **10** (Oote Boe), **12** (Ace Stock Limited), **14** (Westend61/
Manfred J. Bail), **15** (Ace Stock Limited), **18** (Oso Medias),
20 (Gianni Muratore), **21** (vario images GmbH & Co.KG), **22**
(Wm. Baker / GhostWorx Images), **23** (Realimage); Corbis
pp. **8**, **17** (Buddy Mays), **25** (Robert Landau), **26**, **27**; Getty
Images pp. **4** (Retrofile/George Marks), **5** (Photodisc),
6 (Photodisc), **7** (Photographer's Choice/Garry Gay), **19**
(Stone/John Millar), **29**; The Kobal Collection pp. **9**, **24**;
Science Photo Library pp. **11** (Pascal Goet-Gheluck), **13**
(Alain Dex/Publiphoto Diffusion), **16** (Gusto), **28** (Doug
Martin).

Cover photograph reproduced with permission of Corbis/
Zuma/Marianna Day Massey.

Every effort has been made to contact copyright holders
of any material reproduced in this book. Any omissions
will be rectified in subsequent printings if notice is given to
the publishers.

▲In the United Kingdom today, about one person out of four smokes.

Cigarettes are the most common way people smoke tobacco. Smoking cigarettes can give you bad breath, stain your teeth, and make your clothes and hair smell. Smoking is also bad for your health.

What Is Tobacco?

▲ China is the largest grower of tobacco in the world.

Tobacco is a plant that is grown in many parts of the world. It is related to plants that we eat, such as tomatoes, potatoes, and aubergines. It is also related to plants that contain poison.

Tobacco leaves are dried and used to make cigarettes, cigars, pipe tobacco, chewing tobacco, and **snuff**. All forms of tobacco contain a **drug** called **nicotine**.

◄ Many tobacco products are smoked.

Cigar

Tobacco's history

The first tobacco plants grew wild in North and South America. When Christopher Columbus arrived there in 1492, he saw how important tobacco was to the native people. European sailors tried tobacco, and its use quickly spread throughout the world.

◄ Native Americans smoked tobacco in some religious ceremonies.

◄ Early Hollywood stars often smoked in movies.

At first tobacco was too expensive for most people to buy. Then in the 1880s, a machine was invented that made cigarettes by the thousands. Suddenly many people could afford to buy cigarettes. By the 1950s, smoking was common in many parts of the world.

What happens when you use tobacco?

When someone uses tobacco, **nicotine** quickly enters the bloodstream. Soon it reaches the brain, where it causes special **chemicals** to be released.

▲Smoking can damage your sense of smell.

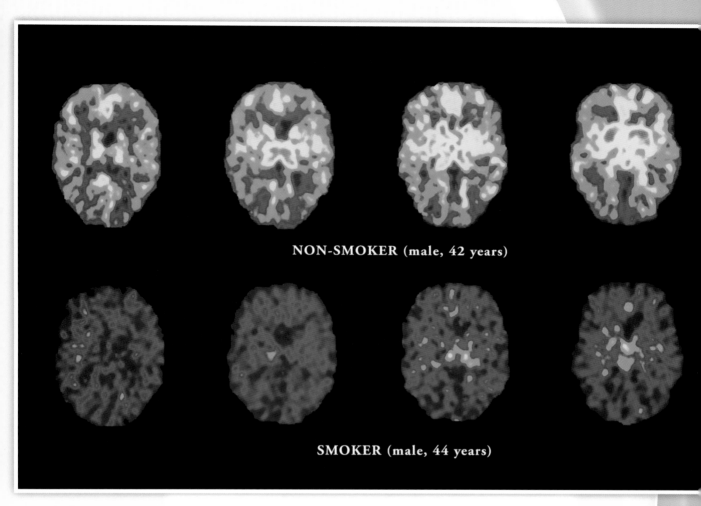

NON-SMOKER (male, 42 years)

SMOKER (male, 44 years)

▲ Smoking changes brain activity over time.

When nicotine sets these chemicals loose, they change the way the smoker feels. The smoker may feel more relaxed.

Tobacco addiction

◄ Smoking irritates the lungs and can make a person cough.

Many people do not like smoking the first time they try it. It can make them feel dizzy or sick. But **nicotine** is **addictive**. It makes people feel as if they cannot live without it.

At first, nicotine can make people feel good. When this begins to fade, people smoke more to bring the feeling back. Over time, smokers get used to nicotine and have to smoke more often for it to **affect** them.

▲Smokers may feel sick when the nicotine level in their body drops.

What is harmful about tobacco?

◄ Cigarette smoke releases a harmful chemical that is also used in rat poison.

Nicotine makes people keep using tobacco, which contains other harmful **chemicals**. One of the most harmful chemicals in tobacco is called benzene. It can cause cancer.

▲ **Carbon monoxide** gas is also given off by cars. It can be deadly in large amounts.

Tobacco smoke contains carbon monoxide, a dangerous gas. It is **absorbed** into the blood and takes up space that carries oxygen. This means smokers cannot breathe as well as they should. Their lungs and heart have to work harder and can be damaged.

Another harmful material in cigarettes is **tar**, the burned particles (pieces) in tobacco smoke. When smokers **inhale**, these particles go deep into their lungs and stick there. Tar can make it harder for smokers to breathe.

◄ Tar can cause diseases such as lung cancer and **emphysema**.

► People who chew tobacco have high rates of mouth cancers, gum disease, and dental problems.

Some people think chewing tobacco is safe because they do not inhale smoke when they use it. They do avoid **tar** and **carbon monoxide**, but the other **chemicals** in tobacco still get into the body.

How does smoking affect other people?

◄ Smoking risks the health of everyone around you.

For a long time, smoking was considered a risk adults took for themselves. Now it is known that people around smokers breathe in the same harmful substances. This is called **passive smoking**.

Passive smokers have a greater risk of lung and heart disease than people who do not live with smoke around them. Children are more likely to have lung problems such as **asthma** and **bronchitis** if they live with smokers.

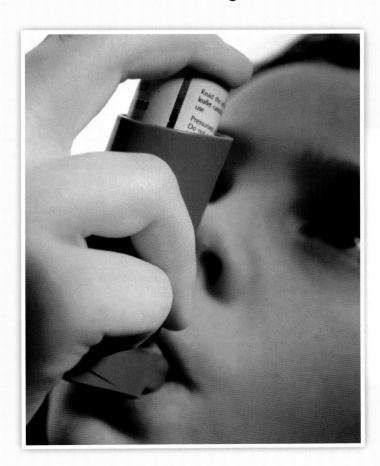

◄ People with asthma must sometimes use an inhaler to help them breathe.

Smoking and the law

Smoking is banned in all public indoor spaces in the United Kingdom. Smoking is also not allowed on aeroplanes in the United Kingdom.

▲Workers who are **addicted** to cigarettes have to take breaks to smoke outside.

▲ Smoking remains popular even though people know it is not good for them.

Selling tobacco products to young people is illegal. However, this law is not always obeyed. That means that young people often have to decide for themselves what is the right thing to do.

Why do kids smoke?

Smoking seriously harms you and others around you

Smoking kills

▲ Tobacco companies must include a health warning on cigarette packets.

Most people who smoke know that it can cause serious health problems. Still, a lot of young people try cigarettes and then become **addicted**.

Some young people start smoking because their friends do it. Some see family members smoking and want to know what it is like. Others may feel it helps them relax.

▶Young people may smoke because they think it makes them look older.

Tobacco companies

Tobacco companies know that smoking is dangerous. However, if they do not get young people to start smoking, the companies will eventually lose all their customers. Some tobacco companies try to make smoking look appealing to young people.

◄ The "Marlboro man" has been used to sell Marlboro cigarettes since 1955.

◀ Johnny Depp played a character who smoked on the television show *21 Jump Street*.

Many governments have banned television advertisements for cigarettes. As a result, cigarette companies have encouraged the creators of television programmes to use characters who smoke. That way, people see actors smoking and may want to start, too.

Trying to give up

◀ Few athletes smoke. They need strong, healthy lungs to perform well.

The sooner someone gives up smoking, the better. The heart and lungs begin to **heal** over time. However, many people try to give up several times before they succeed. It is important to keep trying.

Some people try to give up by first cutting down on the number of cigarettes they smoke each day. Smoking fewer cigarettes can make people **inhale** more deeply with each puff. This can be just as bad as smoking more cigarettes without inhaling as hard.

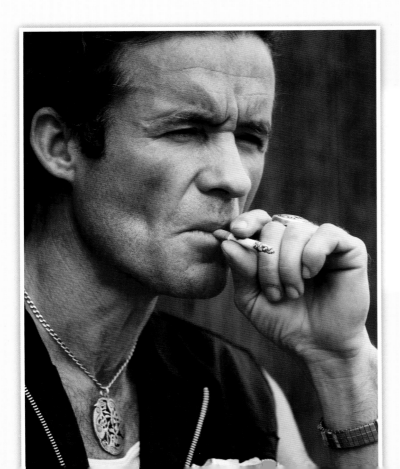

◄ Smoking fewer cigarettes does not always reduce the health risks.

Help with giving up

Giving up smoking can be difficult, but there are ways to get help. Special products that contain safe amounts of **nicotine** can help smokers give up. These include chewing gum and patches that are stuck onto the skin.

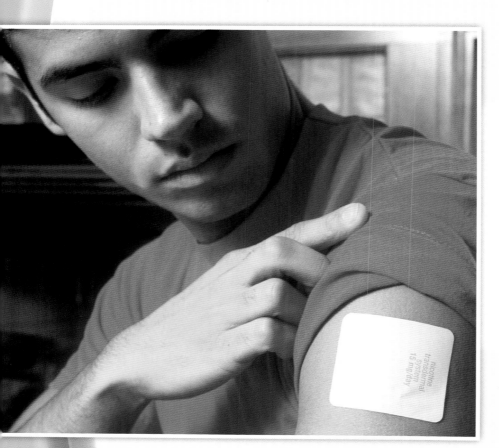

◄ Patches give smokers the nicotine they need to help them give up smoking.

▶ "No Smoking Day" is held to remind people not to smoke.

Friends, family, and special organizations can help people who are struggling to give up smoking. Good places to look for information include Action on Smoking and Health (ASH) and the National Health Service (NHS).

Glossary

affect change

absorb soak in

addictive make a person feel as if they cannot live without it

asthma disease that can cause difficulty breathing

bronchitis swelling in the lungs that can cause breathing problems and severe coughing

carbon monoxide poisonous gas that is often created when something burns

chemical matter that can be created by or is used in scientific processes

drug something that is taken to change how the brain or body works

emphysema lung disease that can cause difficulty breathing and an infection in the lungs

flammable able to catch fire

heal get better

inhale breathe in

nicotine addictive chemical in tobacco products

passive smoking inhaling the smoke from other people's cigarettes

snuff tobacco product that is inhaled through the nose

tar small pieces of solid matter that make up cigarette smoke

Find Out More

Books to read

Talking about smoking by Bruce Sanders (Franklin Watts, 2003)

Harmful Substances by Cath Senker (Hodder Wayland, 2004)

Kate Smokes by Janine Amos (Cherrytree Books, 2002)

Websites

• The NHS has a site dedicated to helping people reject tobacco. (www.gosmokefree.co.uk)

• ASH offers information for people who are worried about smoking. (www.ash.org.uk)

• Quit is a charity that helps people give up smoking. (www.quit.org.uk)

Facts about tobacco

• **Nicotine** is named after Jean Nicot, who lived in the 1500s in France. He thought that tobacco would turn out to be a useful medicine.

• Many house fires are started when a smoker puts a lit cigarette too close to something **flammable**. Forest fires can be started when people throw burning cigarettes into dry grass.

• In the United Kingdom about 114,000 deaths every year are caused by the effects of cigarette smoking.

Index

Contents

Words written in bold, **like this**, are explained in the glossary.

Meet the giraffes

This is Africa, home of giraffes. Giraffes are the tallest **mammals** in the world. To find a giraffe, look for a long neck, long legs, and spots.

▼ *Giraffes are tall enough to peek into a first floor window.*

Wild World

Watching Giraffes in Africa

Deborah Underwood

Heinemann
LIBRARY

www.heinemann.co.uk/library
Visit our website to find out more information about Heinemann Library books.

To order:

 Phone 44 (0) 1865 888066

 Send a fax to 44 (0) 1865 314091

 Visit the Heinemann Bookshop at www.heinemann.co.uk/library to browse our catalogue and order online.

First published in Great Britain by Heinemann Library, Halley Court, Jordan Hill, Oxford OX2 8EJ, part of Harcourt Education. Heinemann is a registered trademark of Harcourt Education Ltd.

Editorial: Nancy Dickmann and Sarah Chappelow
Design: Ron Kamen and edesign
Illustrations: Martin Sanders
Picture Research: Maria Joannou and Christine Martin
Production: Camilla Crask
Originated by Modern Age
Printed and bound in Italy by Printer Trento srl

13 digit ISBN 978 0 431 19084 6 (HB)
10 digit ISBN 0 431 19084 4 (HB)
10 09 08 07 06
10 9 8 7 6 5 4 3 2 1

13 digit ISBN 978 0 431 19087 7 (PB)
10 digit ISBN 0 431 19087 9 (PB)
11 10 09 08 07
10 9 8 7 6 5 4 3 2 1

British Library Cataloguing in Publication Data
Underwood, Deborah
Watching giraffes in Africa. - (Wild world)
599.6'38
A full catalogue record for this book is available from the British Library.

Acknowledgments
The author and publisher are grateful to the following for permission to reproduce copyright material: Ardea pp. **5** (Geoff Trinder), **14** (C. Clem Haagner), **18** (C. Clem Haagner); Corbis pp. **8** (Carl Purcell), **11**, **16** (Nigel J. Dennis), **20**, **26**; FLPA pp. **9** (Minden Pictures), **12** (Mitsuaki Iwago), **17** (Frans Lanting/Minden Pictures), **23** (Frans Lanting/Minden Pictures); Glenda Kapsalis p. **19**; Nature Picture Library pp. **10** (Pete Oxford), **22** (Jeff Foott); NHPA pp. **4** (Martin Harvey), **27** (Rich Kirchner), **29** bottom; Oxford Scientific Films p. **21** (Stan Osolinski); Photographers Direct pp. **24**, **25**; RichardPSmith.com p. **28**; Steve Bloom p. **15**; Still Pictures pp. **7**, **13**. Cover photograph of giraffes reproduced with permission of NHPA (Martin Harvey).

The publishers would like to thank Michael Bright of the BBC Natural History Unit for his assistance in the preparation of this book.

Every effort has been made to contact copyright holders of any material reproduced in this book. Any omissions will be rectified in subsequent printings if notice is given to the publisher. The paper used to print this book comes from sustainable resources.

There are many kinds of giraffes.
Some have light brown spots shaped
like stars. Others are covered with
dark brown patches.

▶▶ *Each type of giraffe has spots that are shaped differently.*

At home in Africa

The **continent** of Africa has many **landscapes**. There are **woodlands** and flat, grassy places called **savannahs**. The savannahs are dotted with trees.

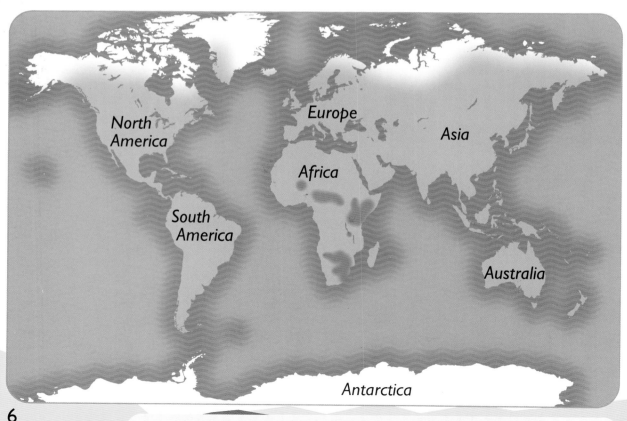

North America

Europe

Asia

Africa

South America

Australia

Antarctica

Key   ● *This colour shows where giraffes live in Africa.*

▲ *Giraffes share the savannah with zebras and other animals.*

The savannahs are warm all year round.
Rains soak the soil for many months
each year. Green plants grow during
this rainy season.

7

There's a giraffe!

A giraffe's long legs and neck can look like tree trunks. They are hard to see because their spots help them blend in with the trees.

▲ *Giraffes are good at hiding, even though they are big.*

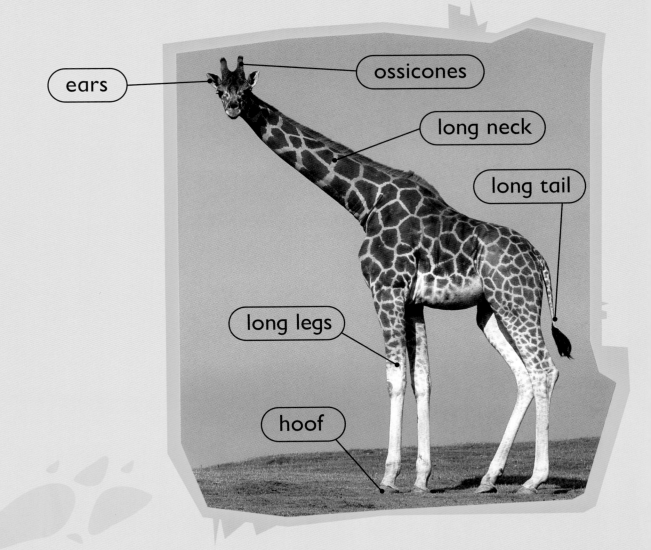

ears

ossicones

long neck

long tail

long legs

hoof

Giraffes have horn-like bumps called **ossicones** on their heads. They flick away flies with their long tails. Each **hoof** is the size of a dinner plate.

Tasty trees

Giraffes eat leaves, seeds, and pods from trees. Animals that eat leaves are called **browsers**. Giraffes like the leaves from **acacia** trees most.

▼ *The acacia trees have very sharp spikes as well as tasty leaves.*

10

There are very few other browsers that can reach these branches.

Giraffes need to eat a lot because they are so big. Their long necks let them pick food that most other animals cannot reach.

How giraffes eat

A hungry giraffe grabs a branch with his long tongue. He pulls the branch into his mouth. Then he uses his teeth to scrape off the leaves.

▼ *Giraffes' hairy lips protect them from the **acacia's** thorns.*

Giraffes swallow their food quickly. They do not chew it much to start with. Later, the food travels back up into their mouths so they can chew it more.

▶▶ Giraffes eat quickly, then chew their food later.

On the move

Walking giraffes move both feet on one side, then both feet on the other. This keeps their legs from getting tangled. Their necks bob up and down with each step.

▼ Giraffes rock from side to side as they walk.

If they see a **predator**, giraffes run away.
Their long legs let them move quickly.
They can **gallop** as fast as a car.

Giraffes would rather run from danger than fight.

The dry season

When the **savannah's** long dry season begins, green grasses turn brown. Plants dry out. The giraffes move closer to lakes and **waterholes**. Green plants still grow there.

▲ *During the dry season, giraffes look for water.*

▼ *A giraffe has to spread out its front legs or bend them to reach water.*

The giraffe must lower its head to drink. With its head down, it is hard to watch for **predators**. Luckily, a giraffe can go for many days without drinking.

Giraffes together

Giraffes move in a group called a **herd**. Some herds are large and some are small. Herds are always changing. The giraffes move from one group to another.

▼ *Herds can be made up of males, or **females** with children, or all three.*

Giraffes are so tall that they can see **predators** from far away. They can spot danger long before it arrives.

⬆ *One or two of the giraffes stand watch while the others rest.*

Giraffe babies

One of the **females** is ready to have a baby. She gives birth standing up. The baby enters the world with a thump as it falls to the ground!

▶▶ *A mother licks her new baby to clean it.*

*Baby giraffes
are as tall as
an adult human.*

Baby giraffes can stand up before they are
one hour old. They drink milk from their
mother. They begin eating plants when
they are about one month old.

Growing up

The baby and mother stay by themselves for a few weeks. This gives the baby a chance to get stronger. Then its mother takes it to meet the **herd**.

Baby giraffes can be born at any time of the year.

▲ This **female** giraffe watches the young
of the herd while their mothers eat.

The mother giraffes take turns caring for
the herd's children. One mother watches
many young giraffes. The other mothers
go off to find food.

Under attack

Leopards, lions, crocodiles, and **hyenas** may attack young giraffes. Lions are the only animals that may try to kill healthy adult giraffes.

▲ *Even lions have a hard time catching a giraffe.*

Giraffes can see a long way. Sneaking up on them is not easy. If a giraffe is attacked, it defends itself by kicking its strong front **hooves**.

▼ *A giraffe's powerful hoof can break the bones of a* **predator***.*

Rainy season

When the rains come, the **savannahs** come alive with new growth. Brown grasses turn green. Soon new **acacia** leaves will sprout on the trees.

▼ *The rains mean new plants and more food for the giraffes.*

▲ *Young giraffes stay with their mothers for at least a year.*

Herds of giraffes spread out across the savannah. After the long dry season, giraffes will once again find tender new leaves to eat.

Tracker's guide

When you want to watch animals in the wild, you need to find them first. You can look for clues they leave behind.

◀◀ A *giraffe's hoofprint is about the same size as a dinner plate.*

◀◀ As they move across the **savannah** looking for food, giraffes leave droppings behind. They look like big acorns.

browse line

▶▶ Sometimes you can tell where giraffes have eaten. A browse line shows how far they have reached to eat.

29

Glossary

acacia thorny tree that grows on savannahs

browser animal that eats leaves

continent the world is divided into seven large areas of land called continents. Each continent is divided into different countries.

female animal that can become a mother when it grows up. Women and girls are female people.

gallop to run quickly on four legs, like a horse

herd group of animals that live and travel together

hoof hard covering on the feet of some animals

hyena wolf-like animal that eats other animals

landscape type of land found in a place. A landscape can have mountains, rivers, forests, and many other things.

male animal that can become a father when it grows up. Men and boys are male people.

mammal animal that feeds its babies with the mother's milk

mate when male and female animals produce young. "Mate" can also mean the partner that an animal chooses to have babies with.

ossicone horn-like bump on a giraffe's head

predator animal that catches and eats other animals for food

savannah area of land mostly covered in sandy soil and grass with some trees and bushes

waterhole pool where animals go to drink water

woodland land with many trees

Find out more

Books

Africa, Leila Foster (Heinemann Library, 2001)

Animal Life Cycles, Anita Ganeri (Heinemann Library, 2005)

Giraffes, Patricia Kendell (Raintree, 2004)

Websites

Visit these websites to find out more amazing facts about giraffes:

http://www.awf.org/wildlives/118

http://www.cmzoo.org/zoocam.html

http://www.kidsplanet.org/factsheets/giraffe.html

http://www.sandiegozoo.org/animalbytes/t-giraffe.html

Disclaimer

All the internet addresses (URLs) given in this book were valid at the time of going to press. However, due to the dynamic nature of the internet, some addresses may have changed, or sites may have ceased to exist since publication. While the author and publishers regret any inconvenience this may cause readers, no responsibility for such changes can be accepted by either the author(s) or the publishers.

Index